The Seven Day Management Course:

A Simple Guide With Effective Strategies To Improve Your Leadership, Management Skills And Your Business

Anthony Ferriss

© 2016

Table of Contents

Introduction

I want to thank you and congratulate you for downloading the book, "The Seven Day Management Course: A Simple Guide With Effective Strategies To Improve Your Leadership, Management Skills, And Your Business".

This book contains proven steps and strategies on how to acquire the necessary skills that are critical for achieving success. The book is based on the traits that are crucial for achieving the desired success and the simple strategies to bring these into the daily routine. These traits can be bifurcated into achievable goals and the set of activities that can be performed daily. The most important part is that all strategies will be charted in a seven-day calendar in such manner that initial period of skipping the plan is reduced to minimal possible end. Every day will be moving on in a progressive way so the reader can develop their interest to keep going with the calendar.

The most important part is the custom calendar preparation that allows the user to create the plans as per his/her needs and availability. Further, the weekly objectives can also be set in a series of steps that collectively concludes as a bigger goal.

Thanks again for downloading this book, I hope you enjoy it!

This document is geared towards providing exact and reliable information in regards to the topic and issue covered. The publication is sold on the idea that the publisher is not required to render an accounting, officially permitted, or otherwise, qualified services. If advice is necessary, legal or professional, a practiced individual in the profession should be ordered.

From a Declaration of Principles which was accepted and approved equally by a Committee of the American Bar Association and a Committee of Publishers and Associations.

The information provided herein is stated to be truthful and consistent, in that any liability, in terms of inattention or otherwise, by any usage or abuse of any policies, processes, or directions contained within is the solitary and utter responsibility of the recipient reader. Under no circumstances will any legal responsibility or blame be held against the publisher for any reparation, damages, or monetary loss due to the information herein, either directly or indirectly.

Breaking the Inertia

The concept of inertia is a quite amazing phenomenon of defining the status of the matter in different relative aspects. Every one of us knows about the basic concepts of physics that are the famous three laws of Newton and the mass energy theory. There is a wide separation among the subjects in terms of humanity and the science stream but when we analyze the things at a higher plane the concepts defined in various streams of science seem to be applicable to the humanities areas and vice versa.

The word inertia bears the wordily meaning of being inactive in common terminology but when we dive deep into the scientific advancement of the rules in basic physics we come across many differential aspects of the word and the applied concept. As per the law of inertia, the object at rest or moving will tend to remain at rest or keep on moving till any external force is applied to it. The same is true in every aspect and applies to various situations in the humanities or the management areas.

The word inertia has a charm on it and it reveals the enigma of the theory of happening. When we think of inertia as a simple word it gives us the sense of inactivity but on the lateral aspects, it relates to the idea of the comfort zone theory. The majority of the people are living in their own inertia and they don't want to break the status quo and want to live in their comfort zone. The subtitle of the introduction of this book "Breaking the Inertia" is not meant to describe the sense of inactivity that you have to fight for acquiring the right traits, but it is relative to the concept of the breaking the comfort zone and building the habit of discarding the routine practices that create hindrances in our progress.

As per the first law of motion, any object in rest or motion continues to be in the position of rest or motion till applied by any external force. The same holds true with our personality traits that are developed over a course of time. The theory of development is quite interesting as when we are a child our state of learning is different from the tendencies that are developed in later years after we reach adulthood. During our childhood and adolescence stages we are a vivid observer and as we reach adulthood the situation changes and we are more prone towards achieving our comfort zone.

This is the basic reason for the development of the passive traits that are critical factors in our success or failure. The whole idea behind breaking the inertia can be simply divided into three stages; first assessment of our passive traits, identifying the opposite traits and strategic planning for breaking the comfort zone. The majority of the people have passive traits that have their roots in the tendency of maintaining the comfort zone. These tend us to divert from the challenges and blocks our risk taking abilities.

Chapter 1 - Seven Day Program:

The idea of the seven-day program for building the capabilities that are essential for becoming a successful leader, manager and business owner is based on the concept of self-assessment and developing custom strategies. Some the basic passive traits that are found in the majority of the people are; being reactive, making pre-assumptions, being lethargic, and more. In the coming chapters of this book, you will come to know about the basic traits that are crucial for being successful as a leader, manager and a business owner.

The whole idea of the seven-day management program is about the simultaneous implementation of the theory of elimination and inculcation of the virtues that makes you successful. The program is about the development of the custom calendar that is focused on adopting the strategies that help in cutting the passive arts and induce the active efforts that are useful in the longer run in every walk of life. It will let you analyze the factors that are responsible for the failure and the effective ways to inculcate the positive traits that will pave your way to success.

In this program, you will run through a rigorous process of self-analysis and strategic thinking that will help you to develop the custom plan for learning the management skills that are critical for success. There are three stages of the program that are a pre-planning stage; implementation stage and review phase that are divided into two, four and one days respectively.

These three stages are defined in accordance with the learning curve that helps us cover all the aspects of skill building which are goal setting, gap assessment, strategy building, ground level training and review. In the preplanning stages, our stress is on the development of the self-assessment skills and analytical abilities that are crucial in setting the achievable goals. Similarly, in the implementation stage, we are developing the strategies to acquire the skills by including the simple habits that help us in developing the desired traits easily.

This stage is focusing on the development of the custom plans that can be applied to inculcate the necessary skills without making it too mechanical. The entire focus is about preparing the custom program that helps in taking us out of the comfort zone without disturbing your routine and present conditions. The basic idea behind the implementation part is to make the learning process easy and custom oriented. The exercises are designed in such a way that it seems to be fun rather than boring lectures.

The third stage is the review of the outcome; that is a sort of assessment which is going to help you in achieving the next set of goals. The program is designed to fit in needs of the people that don't have much time and cannot refer to the lengthy readings prescribed in the management course. It is prepared to involve you in every part of the program by exercises that lead you to assess the zest of the management skills development methodology and help you in learning the process that you may continue on your own without any assistance.

It sets you free from the routine learning process and helps you set your own pace of learning. You may choose one skill at a time and carry on the course for the same. Apart it is not giving you a long list of learning objectives that need to be completed you may go with the desired skills as per your convenience. Above all, it's not time-consuming, except the preplanning process all the implementation part can be completed while you are one the move or while carrying out the other routine works. It is an effort to simplify the management skill development process.

Chapter 2 - Day-One: Breaking the Ice

As we have discussed in the introduction part about the concept of inertia we are about to come out of our comfort zone and start with the brainstorming sessions that are going to be the foundation of the program. In the first two days of preplanning, we will discuss the present situation and our upcoming positions in different roles.

Pre-Planning Stage (2 Days): In this stage, we will be covering the process of self-assessment and situation analysis. This will help you to find out the shortcomings and find out the ways for coming out of the present situations. This can be simply carried out by the pen and paper exercise which you can do on your own. The basic rule for this pre-planning stage is to keep yourself aloof from your role and examine the situation as an external auditor.

This is a kind of self-audit where you need to be brutal towards you and don't let any slip add up. In this process, we will do a simple exercise that is as below. So get ready and take a pen and notebook and sit in a place where nobody is going to disturb you for a couple of hours. It is quite required that you must do this process as religiously as you can because all of your success in the forthcoming stages and program are largely depending on the outcome of these two days. So here we go;

Now start writing about yourself; a brief about you as a person in different roles like; person, manager, leader, businessman, spouse, parent, son or daughter. Don't get confused as we are also adding the roles that are falling in the social zone. It is inevitable for you to build in the success strategies without taking all aspects into consideration because many of the management and business traits are affected by our social and personal life. So try to write as much as you can in as many roles that you can find.

Even if you have worked as a volunteer at a social cause just for one day write it there on the sheet. Once you are done with this then give it a review and see if anything is missing; if yes then add the same.

Now comes the interesting part of the game; this is quite important and fascinating part of the entire program as this gives you the chance to eliminate all the boundaries that confine you as of now. The process is quite simple once you have made a note of all the possible roles that you have played till now we can move on to the next step.

Make a timeline on the paper that depicts four columns for the time against each possible role which will be as below

Role: At Present | After One Year | After Five Years | After Ten Years

This is going to be the benchmark for you during the coming stages of the program. This is a simple goal setting exercise that helps you define the objectives that you want to achieve in the due course of time. Now you have set all the possible roles in present time we will carry-on with the nested set where you have to put the possible progress in a coming time frame.

For example, if you choose your role as a writer in current time then note down the future position that you want to achieve after one year; then after five years and after ten years. This may be something like at present you are writing small articles on different subjects; in the coming one year from now you may want to start as a fiction writer writing short stories and then in the next five years you want to write a few novels and by the completion of ten years you want to be writer that has at least "one of the best sellers" in your name.

In this manner, you can fill the complete chart that defines you in different roles and your ambitions in coming ten years. We are using the word ambition because the goals are yet not defined. In the coming step, we will be discussing achieving the right skills and traits that are critical for achieving success in various roles.

Chapter 3 - Day-Two: Setting the Course of action

This is the second day of the program and we are about to complete the preplanning stage that is going to be the foundation for the real part of the program i.e. the implantation of learning. From this chapter, we will be taking out the zest of the preplanning that will help us to enlist the skills that we are going to acquire in the implementation stage. This is about setting the course of action for the next four days.

Now starts the second step of the pre-planning stage where you have to think a lot. The process is quite simple once you have made the roles as per the different stages of timeline you have to find role models for each stage of your role; you may either choose a single role model for one role in a timeframe or may select different role models for different time frames. Select your role model for each role and put his name in the selected box. This is the typical part of the exercise and needs to be completed with diligence and sound interest. Don't make any vague selection; be careful as it is going to affect your upcoming efforts at larger levels.

 This part of the exercise can be completed in about four hours. We advise you to fill in all the details in one sitting and don't pull on this part from more than four hours for getting an effective outcome. Now you are done with the roles and the role models now comes the third part of preplanning where we will find out the five traits of the successful people i.e. your role models that we will try to inculcate in the coming program. This is most critical part of the preplanning stage as it will define the areas of improvement and custom strategies creation for learning the necessary management skills and leadership traits.

After analyzing the role models sheet you will find some common traits that are present in every successful person. All you have to do is to list these skills and traits of the role models that are essential in making them successful. You may find several traits but, here we will be focusing on the seven top traits that are found in most of the successful persons. We are not going to list these here; this is on your part to find out these traits. Once you are done with this exercise then we will move on the next part of the program; that is five days implementation workshop.

Chapter 4 - Day-Three: Self-assessment vs Anticipation

The day third is the beginning of the second phase of the program that is the implementation of the learning methodologies. In this phase, we are developing the strategies for acquiring the selected skills by developing simple habits and modifying the daily routine. The implementation phase starts with setting up the objectives that we have to achieve.

The exercises related to self-assessment are designed to set the realistic goals and dividing them into achievable objectives. This is quite helpful in making the learning process easy and developing simple methods to acquire the skills with minimal possible efforts. The whole idea is about developing the ways that help us in acquiring the skills without putting pressure so we are least bothered and the only troublesome part that remains to overcome is about coming out of the comfort zone.

The third-day exercise of self-assessment and anticipation is based out on the outcome of the pre-planning efforts. We will begin with the list of the common traits that is derived from the exercises carried out in the pre-planning phase. With this list, we will start on the assessment v/s anticipation process. The core idea of the whole process is to about rationalization of the goals.

Once we have finalized the list of the traits that are deemed to be indispensable in the process of becoming successful leader then we will chart out the traits that are essential for becoming a better manager and then the traits that are critical in getting success in business. Hence, we are having the three roles and the list of the traits that are critical in achieving success in these three roles. It is often observed that there are few common traits that are found to be common in all these three roles.

In this coming exercise, we will be discussing the common five traits of the successful people for an easy understanding of the strategies that are described in the book. It is understood that if you have come up with a long list then you need to evolve the methods on your own and break down the plan into several seven days program. It is needless to say that you can carry on with the strategies defined here to implement the skill learning process.

As discussed, we will continue with the five most common traits of the successful leaders. These are in opposition with the common five trends observed in the common people who want to grow but fail to achieve the desired success. It will help us understand the process of elimination and inculcation of the traits.

We will make two columns on the sheet that will be as below.

Column 1: It will enlist the model traits that you want to achieve based on the list that you have derived from the pre-planning phase.

Column 2: It will be covering your present situation in terms of the skills or the traits as compared with those listed in the first column.

This will help us to figure out the gap between the model and the current conditions which will help us in preparing the plan to achieve the desired objective. The given example will help you understand the same process easily. We will continue with the same goal as described in the first phase of the exercises that states your goal of becoming a successful fiction writer with at least one best seller in your name.

Now when you will analyze the sheets from the second phase from the preplanning steps you will find the skill sets of the successful role models of the writers. So you may land with the qualities that you must inculcate in yourself for becoming a successful writer.

Now the sheet will be read like this;

Column 1: Successful Writer has following traits;

Avid Reader

Keen Observer

Column 2: Yourself in role of writer

Not interested in reading at all

Poor Observation skills

This way you can figure out the gaps within the desired and current skills for becoming a better writer. It will help you to make the strategies and develop your tricks for achieving the desired skills.

Chapter 5 - Day-Four: Setting your own rules

As discussed in the previous chapters we have decided that we will be discussing the five common traits of the successful people and the strategies to achieve those skills. In the chapters 3, 4 and 5, we have understood the process of assessment and gap analysis that helps us in finding the areas of improvement.

Now we have to start with the process of setting objectives and devising the methods for acquiring the skills.

As you all know the seven-day program aims at building the custom plans and strategies for enhancing the skills we will not follow the classical learning methods as found in the management books; but we will evolve the tricks and strategies that favor easy learning without making too much of time. Apart all these methods are based on the smooth transformation from the comfort zone so there are minimal chances of letting the slips add up in your program plan.

Firstly we will list down the common five traits of the successful people then will move on the next process of developing the custom plans for inculcating these skills in ourselves. This will help us in setting our own plan and prepare the strategies that help us in evolving the tricks for adopting these traits. These traits are as below:

Self-Learning

Proactive Approach

Innovative Thinking

Time Management & Prioritization

Self Discipline

As you read on in details about the common traits of the successful people you will come to know that these are quite similar in the leaders in different areas of life irrespective of their field. All of these traits are majorly the skills that are acquired by continued practice and one has to be out of the comfort zone where he /she is suppose to carry on with the routine jobs.

There are no set rules for acquiring these skills and we cannot put the square shaped people in circular box therefore it is inevitable to create whole new ways of preparing the methods of acquiring these traits. The studies of the case studies or the literature based on these skills development can help you in finding the positive aspects of these skills but cannot help you in finding the way to learn the same.

It is the beauty of management that you have to prepare the custom plans for achieving the results on your own. The model plans and cases are suitable to guide on the possibilities but one cannot claim the exact roadmap that is adopted by the other successful people. Therefore, the chapter is defined as setting your own rules. This chapter is based on the two exercises that let you explore your hidden potential as well as help you set your own pace for achieving the desired skills. The first exercise is about finding the multiple solutions to a single problem and the second exercise is about situation analysis.

For Example, we will take the fifth trait Self Discipline which we are supposed to learn. There is enormous online and print material that is available on the said topic and you may find a lot of tricks for achieving the self-discipline but most of these are typically one and the same so there are possibilities that a few of us may get benefited from these but most of us end in frustration. This is not because the tips are incorrect but the basic reason behind the failure is that we are following them blindly without self-assessment.

Therefore; it becomes essential to conduct the self-assessment based on the role models and then find the gap that makes our failure in achieving this trait. Once we are done with the gap analysis the strategies for acquiring the skill comes on its own. As we have discussed earlier in this book the example of the writer also fits in here. From the Traits of a successful writer, we can find that they are avid readers now it can be simply concluded that reading habit requires self-discipline where you have to devote time to reading on a regular basis.

The most of the successful readers are self-disciplined and if you want to be a successful reader then you need to adopt the habits that induce self-discipline like regular reading practice. You have to make your own plan and habit for developing the reading habit and the management literature is not going to help you in doing this. The correlation of the traits with the skills or habits that you want to master is all about setting your own rules.

Chapter 6 - Day-Five: Trial & Error

This is the oldest principle of learning that is used in almost every aspect of learning and development. It is understood that it is the best way to acquire the skills from the very initial level. The tricks for learning the skills that we have derived from the previous chapter are to be tested and implemented during the trial and error phase on the fifth day. On this day, we will find out the multiple methods of learning a single skill. This helps us in finding the best possible method that is suitable for us as well as helps us in devising our own method by mixing one or two.

In the process of skill development, Trial and Error formula is the tool that is most widely used across a small team to a large organization where the learning capabilities of the subjects are falling in a wide range of variations. This helps in fine tuning the key elements in such a manner that every reader can set its own pace for adopting the skill sets. There is one exercise in this chapter that is based on the trial and error concept and derives the facts from the previous chapter where you have to find the multiple solutions for a single problem and the situation analysis.

The facts from the previous chapter help you in making the strategies for achieving the objective as well as developing the new ways of doing the things. The best thing about this exercise is that you can find the multiple ways of doing the single activity which lets you take the liberty of carrying the skill development activities without breaking the old routine or disturbing your work. It also suggests you with the best possible option for acquiring the skills without putting a lot of efforts. This makes it simple for everyone to carry on with the course without investing a lot of time.

We will be continuing with the previous example of the writer where you are striving to adopt the self-discipline trait and fulfill the objective of developing the regular reading habit. Now when we will put this whole outcome in the trial and error formula we will have following situations for developing our own methodology for developing the reading habit. Now when you have equated the leadership trait self-discipline with the habit of regular reading and the skill being an avid reader it becomes obvious that you will try out the different ways to master the habit of regular reading.

Now as per the trial and error method you may try the various methods for reading like you may choose to read the books by visiting the library on the daily basis or you may build your own library, or you can purchase the kindle reader, or you can borrow the books from your friend. So you have found the various possibilities of finding the books to read and similarly you can find the suitable chunk of time that you may devote on a regular basis for reading. Now it's up to you to continue with the easiest way that you can follow on a regular basis to develop the reading habit. In the same manner, the other aspects of trial and error method can be implemented in the different situation and a foolproof method can be adopted by you as per your convenience.

Chapter 7 - Day-Six: No Looking Back

This is the last day of the implementation phase and we are almost done with the course of the seven-day program. Now this is the time to strengthen the basic habits that you have learned so far. It is also the time when we are ready to set the three-week calendar for monitoring our practice. This is the most crucial phase for all the learners as it is the turning point from where you may lose the focus as all the things are clear to you and now you know what you have to do.

From this point, you may develop the thoughts that now we have understood the zest of acquiring the skills so why to bother about continuing and we may do it anytime. If you fall prey to these temptations then all your efforts will be a waste as the tomorrow never comes when it comes to learning new things. So make a strong resolution that you will not give up on this point and will continue for the next three weeks with the method that you have developed for acquiring the desired skills.

The chapter "No looking back" suggests that you must not be blown away with the simplicity of the methods and discontinue just because you think that you may start with the same anytime. This will ruin all your efforts and the possible advantages of the seven-day program will be lost. Now the question is that why this happens? It is a phenomenal thing that when we are able to reveal the secrets we lose interest and end up putting the things off. This is the inertia effect when you reach the status where you find the thing easy you move into your comfort zone and want to stop the process. The simplicity of the program helps you in discovering the various traits and the secrets of success that were unknown to you, but as soon as you become familiar you tend to lose interest in carrying out the process and think that I will do it next time. Therefore, it is strongly advised that you must not look back.

Another important fact that is behind the chapter is that you must not let the slips add up in your plan. Once you fall in the temptation of slipping the routine for a day you may get caught in the trap to miss the routine. This prompts you to let the slip add on and in due course of time you end up discontinuing the routine. The possibilities for missing the routine in temptation are quite big in the first seven days, therefore, we have made the seven days plan to carry out the methods on a regular basis.

Adding to this we strongly advise you to add the three-week calendar for the routines that you have prepared for the outcome of the previous five days. If you continue to carry on these suggestions the possibilities of missing the routine get minimized which in the course of time help you in strengthening the skills that you have acquired from these exercises.

Chapter 8 - Day-Seven: Looking back is essential

This seems to be somewhat contradictory to the previous chapter that is "No Looking Back". But it is not in contrary to the previous chapter but it is the advancement of the said chapter only. The concept of looking back in about keeping your focus on the progress and preparing the plan for reviewing the outcomes of your exercises. The entire exercises that we have carried out so far have resulted in an actionable plan that can be implemented for acquiring the skills in a successful manner.

Now it's the time to review our efforts that's why looking back becomes essential. The process of review is quite simple but it is not just about going through the observation of the efforts but it is aimed to find out the shortcomings as well as discovering the new avenues for improvements. The process of review is quite vast and covers all the aspects of skill development exercise that we have completed so far. The review methodology that we may use can be the simple assessment based on the checking the outcomes with the benchmarks that we have said earlier.

Our review process is not based on the formal assessment as it is large to be conducted by users themselves so it would be easy to cross check the objectives with the benchmarks. For example, if you are working on the objective of developing a regular reading habit for self-discipline then you need to review on the basis of the books that you have read in a week. This will help you to analyze whether you are following the method religiously or not.

Apart it will also let you understand that only reading of the books is not fruitful and it is required that you are making notes of the same. In this way, the review process helps you in understanding the necessary areas for correction in your method also.

Chapter 9 - One More Fact

The most important thing about the seven-day management course that you must know will be detailed in this chapter. The fact that we want to share with the readers is that the basic objective of the course is not about teaching you the management skills development methods or creating the revolutionary product that is going to create a bang in the education sphere but it is all about the analysis of the psychological condition about skill development method and the basic tendencies that most of the readers have. It is also about dealing the tough times that everyone has to face while they start on the plan to acquire new skills. It is observed that the first seven days in the plan of learning new things are quite crucial and requires more efforts by the learner to continue.

The next important thing in the learning and development process is about the psychological changes that are not quite vivid but the expert psychologists can easily understand the behavior pattern. It is observed that the inertia of the comfort zone plays an important role in creating the blockage that retards the learning process for the adults. Apart those in profession or business are quite reluctant towards the change irrespective of their zeal to acquire new skills and to reach the ultimate career heights. This is not because they are not willing to adopt the new methods but it becomes difficult for them to spare more time and get along with the new methods.

The most critical factor that plays an important role in acquiring the new skills is the negative orientation of the person which tends them to oppose the changes. The very first exercise in the program is about to confirm the negative mindset that lets the people prepare the role models in different capacities and select their traits. Once you set the traits that are required then the process of eliminating the opposite trends become easy which would be quite tedious otherwise. All the exercises described in the program are basically the process of revealing our inner strengths that play an important role in developing skills that are critical for being a successful leader.

Chapter 10 - You can do it to

The most common five traits of the successful leaders, managers and business person are the same that we have described in the previous chapter and you can also inculcate those in yourself easily with the methods described in the program. In this chapter, we will try to share some handy tips for acquiring the desired traits for becoming successful.

Self-Learning: It is the most promising trait that plays in every situation. The successful person knows that our brain also requires feed and the good books are food for our mind. So if you want to acquire the first trait develop the habit of reading on a regular basis. This will help you in learning many things that you may not learn otherwise. It is the best things that you may do even you are alone and get benefited without many efforts.

Proactive Approach: This is the simplest method that can change your orientation at larger levels. The proactive person has confidence in himself and he may create the favorable situation by his efforts. The easiest method of becoming proactive that you may start on immediately without involving anyone is to increase your walking speed. It is observed that when you start walking at a faster speed your confidence boosts up automatically and it helps you in becoming proactive. This is a must try the trick that you can test at any time.

Innovative Thinking: When it comes to innovative thinking the first thing that strikes our mind is about the discovery of new things and so on but it is not actually the case the concept is about creative thinking that allows you to think of the multiple solutions to a single problem. The best method of developing the innovative thinking is to start with the pen and paper exercise on daily basis. Just choose one topic and write a write-up of 400+ words on a daily basis on the same topic. It will soon become clear that you need to develop the habit of reading for adding a new dimension to your thinking. This way you may easily acquire the skill of innovative thinking.

Time Management & Prioritization

This is one of the most debated topics that are discussed among the management sphere in many ways. It is quite essential for you to get in the sense of time management and prioritization. This helps you in overcoming many issues as well as let you become successful in every manner. The simplest exercise that will help you in learning time management is about listing the pending matters with you. The day you are left with no pending due to your own at the time you go to sleep your journey to success has started.

Self-Discipline

It is an essential part of any success strategy. Once you take control over yourself the rising begins. The simplest method of getting self-disciplined is to fix the time to rise in the morning. Do this with the help of the alarm clock if you cannot manage on your own. If you succeed in making a habit of rising at a fixed time then you can practice self-discipline easily.

All the methods given above can be either practiced as separate or you may start on with them simultaneously.

Chapter 11 - Build your own calendar

This is the best thing for the entire program that we have detailed till now. It is going to be the best part of all the exercises as it is the report card that shows your daily progress at a glance. It is quite simple to prepare the calendar for tracking your progress. It is just like the simple calendar that has the objective on the left-hand side and the number of days in the right-hand columns starting from 01 to 31. Just note the objective on the first column of the calendar and mark the number of days till you are going to complete the exercise.

This is also useful as a reminder for you to carry on the activities in a regular manner. Apart you can also add one more column that details about the progress in a quantifiable manner if you are breaking the objective in different segments. Along with this, you can also add the role models and the number of traits that you are willing to adopt from the role model. This is going to help you in finding the number of days that are required for achieving all the necessary skills that your role model has for becoming successful. It is the easiest possible chart that gives you the track record of everything on the single sheet.

The main objective behind the development of the calendar is to ensure that you are not skipping the important traits as well as completing the exercises on a timely basis. This is the tool that acts as mentor and guide for completing the exercises in due time. Apart the calendar you may also create the trait charts and the goals that you want to achieve from the exercises described in the previous chapters. This may support you as the easy handbook for memorizing the goals and the traits that you want to acquire from the role models. It is the easiest way of reminding you on a daily basis to work for achieving the lifetime goals in a simple manner. We strongly advise you to prepare these charts and calendar for getting the maximum of your efforts.

Conclusion

Thank you again for downloading this book!

The entire program is aimed at building the orientation of the reader in such a way that they are inclined towards achieving the necessary skills that are critical to achieving success in any walk of life. This will surely help you in defining the core areas where you require improvement and devise the necessary methods for acquiring the requisite skills. The program is not aimed to teach or preach you for achieving the skills or boast about the advantages that these skills which you may have, but it focuses on the areas that are critical in making anyone successful.

It highlights the simple processes that you may carry out on your own for self-assessment and conduct the gap analysis for achieving the desired skills within defined time frame. The most important part of the book is the methodology that it follows for developing the skills without adding a lot of fuss. All you need to do is to sit with the outcome of the gap analysis and find the best possible ways to achieve the desired results. Along with this, you will find the most common five traits that are indispensably present in the successful people. These traits can also help you in achieving the best possible results.

The best part of the book is about the development of the custom calendar and the charts that help you in charting the progress on daily basis. In the entire program is suitable for those who don't want to get trapped in the jargons used in the skill development literature but provide you with the simple insights that are useful in making custom strategies for acquiring the skills for making you successful without wasting a lot of time and efforts. It gives you the key to successful skill development plan.

The next step is to apply what you have learned, put everything into action and change for the better. Take action now what you have learned and try to be one of the few who makes and not the many who just talk.

Finally, if you enjoyed this book, then I'd like to ask you for a favor, would you be kind enough to leave a review for this book on Amazon? It'd be greatly appreciated!

Click here to leave a review for this book on Amazon!

Thank you and good luck!

Before You Go

If you like this book would you be a kind enough to leave a favorable review?

Every review helps and I want to make sure that I arrange quality information and value to help my readers the best possible way. Your feedback and opinion is very important!

Best Wishes,

Anthony Ferriss.

Preview Of: "The 7-Day Mindfulness For Beginners Challenge: A Simple Step-By-Step Guide To Living In The Present Moment, For Transforming Your Leadership And Your Life".

Chapter 1: Introducing mindfulness

Returning to true self

Life is supposed to be mindful, completely open to the experiences without the feeling of conflict. Because where there is conflict, there is disharmony. Where there is disharmony, there is sorrow...there is suffering. Apparently, mindfulness is a skill people develop to improve every aspect of their lives. But once you learn and realize the intrinsic principals of mindfulness, you will also know that mindfulness is our true nature. It was there ever since we were born. But as we grew up, we picked up all those negative information from people along the way. We developed false perceptions, beliefs, prejudices and allowed them to shape our world, our destiny. We deviated from the mindful way and choose a life of disharmony. Returning to mindfulness is like returning home, returning to our true self.

A brief history

Mindfulness is actually an ancient Buddhist meditation Vipassana, simplified. The word mindfulness is the translation of Pali word 'Sati'. To make this meditation more accessible for the non-Buddhists and common audiences, the pioneers of Mindfulness stripped off its religious aspects and made it simple and comprehensible for everyone. Back in 70's, Jon Kabrat-Zinn, a professor of medicine at the University of Massachusetts medical school, started a campaign to popularize his own version of 'Vipassana,' which he termed as 'mindfulness', as an effective approach for dealing with stress, anxiety, depression and few other mental ailments. Inspired by a Zen missionary, Philip Kapleau, he extensively studied Buddhist philosophy, educated himself at 'Insight Meditation Society', and eventually taught there. His mindfulness movement quickly gained popularity among the psychotherapists, doctors, and communities interested in holistic approach to treat and cure various physical and mental disorders.

Understanding mindfulness

In simple term, mindfulness is about being completely present in this very moment. But there is more to it. If the mind tries to stay present, the pursuit may turn into a struggle. Say, for example, you are in pain; and if you are trying to stay present with the pain without the spontaneous acceptance, the pain will become unbearable. Because you are forcing your mind to stay with a sensation which it perceives as unwanted and uncomfortable, and actively wants to escape. Mind aspires to the feeling of comforts and tries to escape feelings, which it views as unpleasant. But life is a journey... there will be moments of joy and moments of sorrow, despair and agony. Remaining present in this very moment involves accepting moment the way it is. It is about embracing the reality without judgment and criticism. Mindfulness is a destination, which the mind seeks throughout its life. When the acceptance takes place, life becomes full of bliss.

Why being mindful?

In the beginning, mindfulness was introduced as a treatment approach and a cure for various illnesses. But mindfulness doesn't just cure disease; it heals the soul and brings harmony. Despite having fame and fortune, some people found the joy of living, for the first time in their life once they learned the mindful way. Mindfulness may offer you innumerable benefits, but the biggest gift of mindfulness is bliss. If the mind remains in a blissful state, it enjoys the inner harmony. When there is harmony in the inner world, there is harmony in the world outside. However, if the readers are looking for other benefits of mindfulness, like if it can bring riches, my answer will be yes it can, if you learn the mindful way of attaining riches. To summarize the benefits of mindfulness, I would like to highlight three key areas of life where mindfulness can play a pivotal role: success, healing, and self-realization.

Is mindfulness just a meditation?

The journey of mindfulness may start with meditation, but in time it becomes an essential law of living. Mindfulness is a state of mind and a way of living. The practitioner will find inner-peace in few days from practicing meditation, but gradually this peace would envelop his whole life and his whole life will transform into meditation. He will walk mindfully, talk mindfully, eat mindfully, and even sleep mindfully. From meditation, mindfulness will turn into a way of life. That is our goal. We will start with meditation because in this way we can prepare the mind more efficiently. With the methods of meditation we can calm the unsettled mind, and when the mind becomes calm, it becomes docile and better prepared for transforming itself. In the next chapter, we will discuss how to prepare ourselves for practicing mindfulness and the basic mindfulness meditation.

The seven-day program

This book is an absolute beginners' guide for learning mindfulness meditation within just a week, following a step-by-step process. The chapters were designed sequentially and each chapter was built on what was covered in the previous chapter. Therefore it is recommended not to skip any chapter. We will start with some healthy practices and breathe exercises to prepare ourselves for the meditation. Then we will move towards the meditation part. Theoretical understanding is paramount here. Sometimes it takes a while to fully grasp the theory, and once it is completely understood, the practical aspects become very easier. You may find repetitions of some ideas throughout the book, but it is important. The same idea has to be reinforced in many occasions to develop your cognitive ability. As I have mentioned earlier, mindfulness is not merely a meditation, it is a way of life. The practice will eventually change the chemistry of our brain and transform our world. Our cognitive transformation will initiate this process. But simply reading the theories won't do much help, you have to actively practice and learn through self-realization. After a few chapters on meditation, we will learn how to practice mindfulness in everyday activities, so that our whole life eventually becomes mindful. Within seven days we will cover all the major areas of life we can deal in the mindful way. Although it will be impractical to guarantee that you will turn into an adept accomplishing the 7 days course. However, if you are a sincere practitioner, 7 days should be enough to elevate you to a level, from where you can make a journey towards profound understanding and great achievements.